~A BINGO BOOK~

# Ancient Rome Bingo Book

## COMPLETE BINGO GAME IN A BOOK

Veduta dell' Anfiteatro Flavio, detto il Colosseo

Reproduction of a Drawing by Giovanni Battista Piranesi (1720-1778)

**Written By Rebecca Stark**

ISBN 978-0-87386-478-7

**Educational Books 'n' Bingo**

Printed in the U.S.A.

# ANCIENT ROME BINGO
## Directions

**INCLUDED:**

List of Terms

Templates for Additional Terms and Clues

2 Clues per Term

30 Unique Bingo Cards

Markers

1. **Either cut apart the book or make copies of ALL the sheets. You might want to make an extra copy of the clue sheets to use for introduction and review. Keep the sheets in an envelope for easy reuse.**

2. Cut apart the call cards with terms and clues.

3. Pass out one bingo card per student. There are enough for a class of 30.

4. Pass out markers. You may cut apart the markers included in this book or use any other small items of your choice.

5. Decide whether or not you will require the entire card to be filled. Requiring the entire card to be filled provides a better review. However, if you have a short time to fill, you may prefer to have them do the just the border or some other format. Tell the class before you begin what is required.

6. There are 50 topics. Read the list before you begin. If there are any topics that have not been covered in class, you may want to read to the students the topic and clues before you begin.

7. There is a blank space in the middle of each card. You can instruct the students to use it as a free space or you can write in answers to cover topics not included. Of course, in this case you would create your own clues. (Templates provided.)

8. Shuffle the cards and place them in a pile. Two or three clues are provided for each topic. If you plan to play the game with the same group more than once, you might want to choose a different clue for each game. If not, you may choose to use more than one clue.

9. Be sure to keep the cards you have used for the present game in a separate pile. When a student calls, "Bingo," he or she will have to verify that the correct answers are on his or her card AND that the markers were placed in response to the proper questions. Pull out the cards that are on the student's card keeping them in the order they were used in the game. Read each clue as it was given and ask the student to identify the correct answer from his or her card.

10. If the student has the correct answers on the card AND has shown that they were marked in response to the *correct questions,* then that student is the winner and the game is over. If the student does not have the correct answers on the card OR he or she marked the answers in response to *the wrong questions,* then the game continues until there is a proper winner.

11. If you want to play again, reshuffle the cards and begin again.

**Have fun!**

# TERMS INCLUDED

AQUEDUCTS

ASSEMBLIES

AUGUSTUS

AURORA

BACCHUS

BATHS

JULIUS CAESAR

CERES

CICERO

CIRCUS MAXIMUS

COLOSSEUM

CONSTANTINE I

DIANA

EPITHETS

ETRUSCANS

FAUNS

FORUM

GREEKS

HADRIAN'S WALL

HORACE

INSULAE (Insula, singular)

JANUS

JUNO

JUPITER

JUSTINIAN

LEGION

MARS

MERCURY

MINERVA

MOSAICS

NEPTUNE

OVID

PANTHEON

PATRICIANS

PAX ROMANA

PLEBIANS

PLUTO

POMPEII

PUNIC WARS

REPUBLIC

ROADS

ROMAN EMPIRE

ROMULUS

SENATORS

SULLA

VENUS

VESTA

VIRGIL

VULCAN

WARDROBE

Ancient Rome Bingo

# Additional Terms

Choose as many additional terms as you would like and write them in the squares. Repeat each as desired.
Cut out the squares and randomly distribute them to the class.
Instruct the students to place their square on the center space of their card.

|  |  |  |  |  |
|---|---|---|---|---|
|  |  |  |  |  |
|  |  |  |  |  |
|  |  |  |  |  |
|  |  |  |  |  |
|  |  |  |  |  |
|  |  |  |  |  |

Ancient Rome Bingo

# Clues for
# Additional Terms

Write three clues for each of your additional terms.

_____

1.

2.

3.

_____

1.

2.

3.

_____

1.

2.

3.

_____

1.

2.

3.

_____

1.

2.

3.

_____

1.

2.

3.

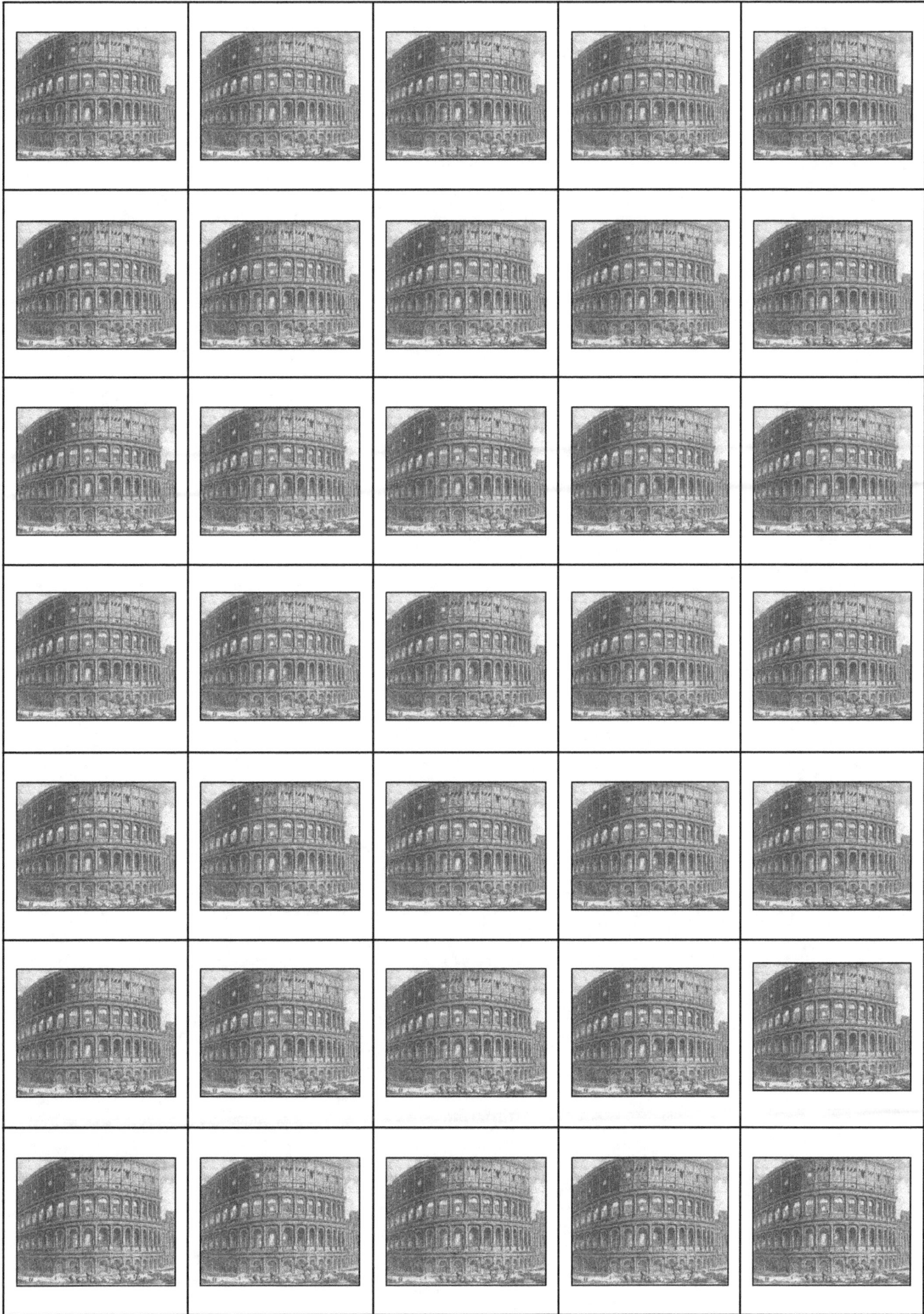

## Aqueducts

1. From 312 BCE to 226 CE eleven of these structures were built to bring water to Rome from areas up to about 60 miles away.
2. They are considered one of the greatest engineering feats of the ancient world.
3. Only about 30 of their 260 miles consisted of the huge arched structures we think of when these are mentioned.

## Assemblies

1. ___ were the legislative branch of the Republic.
2. The oldest was the *comitia curiata*, but by the late Republic its functions were mostly ceremonial.
3. The *comitia centuriata* was one; it elected consuls, praetors, and censors; declared war; and served as court of appeal for citizens sentenced to death. The *comitia tributa* elected other magistrates.

## Augustus

1. Also known as Octavian, he was the first Roman Emperor. He was a great patron of the arts and his reign became known as the Golden Age of Roman Literature.
2. He became emperor in 43 BCE when Julius Caesar was assassinated.
3. In 31 BCE he defeated Antony and Cleopatra at Actium and became undisputed ruler of Rome.

## Aurora

1. She was the goddess of dawn.
2. Her Greek counterpart was Eos.
3. This goddess renewed herself every morning and flew across the sky, announcing the arrival of her brother, the sun.

## Bacchus

1. He was the god of wine.
2. His Greek equivalent was Insulae.
3. The celebrations held in his honor became so unruly that the Senate forbade them in 186 BCE.

## Baths

1. The facilities resembled modern spas.
2. Even wealthy people who had them in their villas often frequented public ones.
3. These were an important part of the people's daily lives. In addition to their normal hygienic functions, they provided opportunities for sports and recreation.

## Julius Caesar

1. He joined with Pompey and Crassus in a coalition now called "The First Triumvirate."
2. He conquered Gaul in 51 BCE and was elected consul in 49 BCE.
3. He was killed by a group of conspirators that included his friend Brutus on March 15, 44 BCE.

## Ceres

1. She was the daughter of Saturn, god of agriculture and the harvest. She was the goddess of agriculture, grain, and a mother's love.
2. Her Greek equivalent was Demeter.
3. When her daughter Proserpina was with her husband Pluto in the Underworld, this goddess grieved and the earth suffered.

## Cicero

1. This statesman is considered by many to be Rome's greatest orator.
2. He named his *Philippics,* in which he argued for the restoration of the Republic, after the speeches given by Horace against Philip II of Macedonia.
3. This great orator was killed in 43 BCE as part of Antony's proscription.

Ancient Rome Bingo

## Circus Maximus

1. This ancient hippodrome was a venue for mass entertainment.
2. Chariot races, horse races, and performances to commemorate important events of the empire were held there.
3. Chariot races were the most important events held there and its track could hold up to 12 chariots.

| | |
|---|---|
| **Colosseum**<br>1. This elliptical amphitheater is a great work of Roman architecture and engineering.<br>2. This amphitheater could seat about 50,000 spectators.<br>3. Gladiatorial contests and other public spectacles were held there. | **Constantine I**<br>1. He was the first Roman Emperor to accept Christianity.<br>2. He issued the Edict of Milan in 313 in which he proclaimed religious tolerance throughout the Empire.<br>3. He created a new central city for the Roman Empire at Byzantium. That city was later named after him and is now called Istanbul. |
| **Diana**<br>1. She was the goddess of the hunt.<br>2. Her equivalent in Greek mythology was Artemis.<br>3. She eventually replaced Luna as the moon goddess. | **Epithets**<br>1. Many major Roman deities had several of these names, each representing a different role or aspect.<br>2. Jupiter Caelestis, or Heavenly Jupiter, and Jupiter Pluvius, or Sender of Rain, were two of Jupiter's.<br>3. Juno Regina, or Juno the Queen, and Juno Moneta, or Juno Who Warns, were two of Juno's. |
| **Etruscans**<br>1. They were members of a pre-Roman civilization.<br>2. Veii was on of their cities. It fell to Rome in 396 BCE.<br>3. They were eventually absorbed by the Romans, who adopted many of their ways. | **Fauns**<br>1. These guardian spirits had horns; they looked like goats below the waist and humans above it.<br>2. They were similar to the Greek satyrs, but unlike the satyrs who had human feet, they had goat feet.<br>3. These forest deities accompanied the god Faunus. |
| **Forum**<br>1. It was the marketplace, business district and civic center of ancient Rome.<br>2. It was located between the Palatine Hill and the Capitoline Hill.<br>3. Temples, a senate house and law courts were built on it. | **Greeks**<br>1. Although the Romans borrowed their deities, they retained many of their own beliefs. For example, each household had protective deities of the hearth, called Lares and Penates.<br>2. They influenced the Romans in art, literature, banking, philosophy and more.<br>3. Many, such as Cato the Elder, were wary of their influence and thought it would bring doom. |
| **Hadrian's Wall**<br>1. This fortification was the northernmost boundary of the Roman Empire until the beginning of the fifth century.<br>2. The Romans built it across northern Britain to protect it from the Picts. Construction began in 122 CE.<br>3. This fortification went from the North Sea to the Irish Sea.<br>Ancient Rome Bingo | **Horace**<br>1. He was the most important lyric poet during the time of Augustus.<br>2. He is known for his *Odes, Satires* and *Epistles.*<br>3. Some of the Latin phrases used by this lyric poet are in use today. An example is *carpe diem,* or "seize the day."<br>**© Barbara M. Peller** |

| | |
|---|---|
| **Insulae (Insula, singular)**<br>1. They were tenement-like apartment buildings where many people lived.<br>2. These 6- or 7-storey buildings had no running water.<br>3. Generally speaking, these apartment buildings were poorly constructed and often burned or collapsed. | **Janus**<br>1. He was the god of gates, doors, doorways, beginnings, and endings.<br>2. Our first month is named after this god of beginnings.<br>3. This god was depicted with two heads facing in different directions. |
| **Juno**<br>1. She was the patron goddess of Rome and the Roman Empire. As the wife of Jupiter, she was called *Regina,* or queen.<br>2. Her Greek counterpart was Hera.<br>3. The women held an annual festival called the Matronalia in her honor. | **Jupiter**<br>1. He was the patron god of Rome and the husband of Juno.<br>2. The largest planet in our solar system is named for him.<br>3. His Greek equivalent was Zeus and, like him, wielded a thunderbolt. |
| **Justinian I**<br>1. He was emperor of the Eastern Roman Empire from 527 to 565.<br>2. The devastating plague that affected the Byzantine Empire in 541 and 542 was later named after him.<br>3. This Byzantine Emperor issued a collection of fundamental works in jurisprudence, now known as the *Corpus Juris Civilis*, or "Body of Civil Law." | **Legion**<br>1. It usually refers to the heavy infantry, the basic military unit of the late Roman Republic and the Roman Empire.<br>2. This military unit was made up of cohorts, each divided into centuries; each century was led by a centurion.<br>3. Sometimes the word is used to refer to the entire Roman army. |
| **Mars**<br>1. He was the god of war.<br>2. At first he was the god of fertility and vegetation. As the Roman Empire began to expand, he came to be identified with the Greek god Ares.<br>3. To the Roman legions, he was the most important god after Jupiter. | **Mercury**<br>1. This messenger god was also the god of trade and commerce.<br>2. His Greek counterpart was Mars.<br>3. Like Mars, he wore a winged hat and winged sandals and carried the caduceus. |
| **Minerva**<br>1. She was the goddess of warriors, poetry, wisdom, medicine, commerce, and crafts.<br>2. Her Greek equivalent was Athene.<br>3. Her festival, the Quinquatria, was celebrated mostly by artisans. | **Mosaics**<br>1. The Romans made them by arranging small pieces of stone into a mortar background to create a pattern or picture.<br>2. They were often used to decorate floors.<br>3. The gods, the exploits of the heroes, nature, and daily life were among the subjects depicted in them. |

| | |
|---|---|
| **Neptune**<br>1. Brother of Jupiter and Pluto, he was the god of water and the sea.<br>2. He is similar to the Greek Poseidon, but also has many elements of the Etruscan god Nethuns.<br>3. This god was associated as fresh water as well as sea water. | **Ovid**<br>1. He, Virgil and Horace are considered by many to be the most important poets of Latin literature.<br>2. Much of what we know about Greco-Roman mythology comes from his *Metamorphoses,* a narrative poem in fifteen books.<br>3. His *Metamorphoses* focuses on transformations, such as Arachne's transformation into a spider. |
| **Pantheon**<br>1. It was originally built as a temple to all the gods of ancient Rome.<br>2. It means "temple of all the gods."<br>3. The current building was completed in 128 CE during Hadrian's reign. For over 1,700 years it had the largest unreinforced solid concrete dome in the world. | **Patricians**<br>1.These rich landowners often had a house in the city and a villa in the country.<br>2. They were the elite aristocracy. Their assembly was called the Senate.<br>3. At first they were the only ones who could hold public office. |
| **Pax Romana**<br>1. It refers to the long period of relative peace established by Augustus.<br>2. It generally refers to about 27 BCE to 180 CE when there were no major civil wars or invasions.<br>3. In spite of its name, there were some smaller battles and wars of conquest during this time. | **Plebians**<br>1. They comprised all those Romans who were not Patricians or slaves.<br>2. Although they would never be considered patricians, some did become *nobiles,* or nobles, and many became very wealthy.<br>3. They gained an important power when the Tribune of the Plebs was granted the right to *veto.* |
| **Pluto**<br>1. He was the god of the Underworld and the brother of Jupiter and Neptune.<br>2. His Greek counterpart was Hades.<br>3. When his wife Proserpina was with him and not her mother, Ceres, the Earth suffered. | **Pompeii**<br>1. This city was buried when Mount Vesuvius erupted in 79 CE.<br>2. Along with Herculaneum and other nearby towns, it was destroyed by the eruption of Mount Vesuvius.<br>3. This town near Naples, Italy, has been excavated and has given us a lot of information about life in ancient Rome in the first century. |
| **Punic Wars**<br>1. These conflicts were between Rome and Carthage.<br>2. Scipio Africanus the Elder defeated Hannibal of Carthage in the second one.<br>3. As a result of the second of these wars, Rome gained parts of northern Africa, Spain, and much of the western Mediterranean. It was now an international empire. | **Republic**<br>1. It was established in 510 BCE.<br>2. Its offices included consul, praetor, censor, aedile and quaestor and sometimes a dictator.<br>3. Its assemblies included the Senate, the *comitia curiata,* the *comitia centuriata,* the *concilium plebis* and the *comitia tributa.*<br>3. Its *comitia centuriata* elected two top officials called consuls. |

Ancient Rome Bingo

© **Barbara M. Peller**

| **Roads** | **Roman Empire** |
|---|---|
| 1. The Romans called them *viae.*<br>2. They enabled the Romans to move armies and goods and to communicate from one part of their empire to another.<br>3. They eventually spanned 53,819 miles, or 85,004 kilometers. | 1. Augustus is considered its first emperor. Marcus Aurelius was its last.<br>2. Historian Edward Gibbon wrote about its decline and fall.<br>3. At its height it spanned an area of about 2.5 million square miles, or 6.5 million square kilometers. |
| **Romulus** | **Senators** |
| 1. This mythological founder of Rome killed his brother Remus and became Rome's first king.<br>2. According to the legend, he and his twin brother Remus were nursed by a she-wolf after being set adrift in the Tiber in a basket.<br>3. In Roman mythology, he and his brother Remus were sons of Mars, the god of war. | 1. They had a great deal of power because they served for life.<br>2. Originally they were patrician advisors to the king.<br>3. Their power declined in the late republic because of the reforms of the tribunes Tiberius and Gaius Gracchus. |
| **Sulla** | **Venus** |
| 1. In 82 or 81 BCE he was appointed dictator by the Senate and was given complete power.<br>2. He was the first to issue a proscription, or official public listing of enemies of the state.<br>3. As dictator, he carried out a reign of terror. Enemies who were put on his proscription lists were executed and their heads were displayed in the Forum. | 1. She was the Roman goddess of love, beauty and fertility.<br>2. Her Greek equivalent was Aphrodite.<br>3. She is the only goddess to have a planet named for her. |
| **Vesta** | **Virgil** |
| 1. She was the goddess of the hearth, home and family.<br>2. It was the task of the Vestal Virgins, her female priests, to maintain her sacred fire.<br>3. This goddess was especially important to women because the hearth was where food was prepared. | 1. This Roman poet is best known for the epic poem, the *Aeneid.*<br>2. His epic Latin poem, the *Aeneid,* tells the legendary story of the Trojan hero Aeneas.<br>3. In his epic poem, Juno tries to prevent the Aeneas from reaching Italy. |
| **Vulcan** | **Wardrobe** |
| 1. He was the god of both beneficial and destructive fire, including that of volcanoes.<br>2. His Greek counterpart was Mercury.<br>3. His forge was located beneath Mount Etna. | 1. It was designed to reveal the social status of its wearer. Only male citizens could include a toga in theirs.<br>2. A senator's consisted of a white toga, purple bands and boots.<br>3. A woman's included a stola and a palla. |

Ancient Rome Bingo

© Barbara M. Peller

# Ancient Rome Bingo

| Roman Empire | Aqueducts | Bacchus | Justinian | Circus Maximus |
|---|---|---|---|---|
| Julius Caesar | Assemblies | Venus | Pantheon | Pax Romana |
| Aurora | Virgil |  | Plebians | Vulcan |
| Wardrobe | Forum | Sulla | Mosaics | Patricians |
| Pluto | Horace | Jupiter | Vesta | Mercury |

# Ancient Rome Bingo

| | | | | |
|---|---|---|---|---|
| Wardrobe | Aurora | Minerva | Romulus | Juno |
| Patricians | Etruscans | Cicero | Forum | Neptune |
| Diana | Horace | | Greeks | Sulla |
| Pompeii | Roads | Virgil | Republic | Circus Maximus |
| Pax Romana | Venus | Jupiter | Julius Caesar | Vesta |

Ancient Rome Bingo: Card No. 2

# Ancient Rome Bingo

| Horace | Sulla | Etruscans | Mosaics | Aurora |
|---|---|---|---|---|
| Patricians | Assemblies | Constantine I | Aqueducts | Legion |
| Forum | Venus |  | Neptune | Augustus |
| Virgil | Diana | Pluto | Pompeii | Minerva |
| Vesta | Julius Caesar | Jupiter | Republic | Juno |

# Ancient Rome Bingo

| Virgil | Neptune | Bacchus | Julius Caesar | Juno |
|--------|---------|---------|---------------|------|
| Mars | Ceres | Aqueducts | Romulus | Aurora |
| Plebians | Pompeii |  | Mercury | Justinian |
| Sulla | Hadrian's Wall | Venus | Jupiter | Cicero |
| Colosseum | Pax Romana | Baths | Vesta | Vulcan |

Ancient Rome Bingo: Card No. 4

© Barbara M. Peller

# Ancient Rome Bingo

| | | | | |
|---|---|---|---|---|
| Pax Romana | Circus Maximus | Forum | Cicero | Julius Caesar |
| Mars | Sulla | Constantine I | Greeks | Assemblies |
| Bacchus | Vulcan | | Pantheon | Insulae |
| Mercury | Juno | Roman Empire | Republic | Epithets |
| Etruscans | Jupiter | Aurora | Virgil | Plebians |

Ancient Rome Bingo: Card No. 5

# Ancient Rome Bingo

| Augustus | Neptune | Minerva | Juno | Vulcan |
|---|---|---|---|---|
| Mosaics | Forum | Epithets | Aqueducts | Aurora |
| Romulus | Colosseum | | Ceres | Greeks |
| Jupiter | Pluto | Republic | Baths | Bacchus |
| Patricians | Cicero | Roman Empire | Plebians | Hadrian's Wall |

© Barbara M. Peller

# Ancient Rome Bingo

| Roman Empire | Neptune | Insulae | Sulla | Etruscans |
|---|---|---|---|---|
| Patricians | Juno | Horace | Assemblies | Mars |
| Minerva | Justinian |  | Greeks | Ceres |
| Virgil | Pompeii | Constantine I | Wardrobe | Diana |
| Jupiter | Julius Caesar | Republic | Baths | Augustus |

# Ancient Rome Bingo

| Plebians | Neptune | Fauns | Mosaics | Ceres |
|---|---|---|---|---|
| Mars | Bacchus | Romulus | Vulcan | Cicero |
| Hadrian's Wall | Punic Wars | | Juno | Circus Maximus |
| Vesta | Virgil | Wardrobe | Colosseum | Pompeii |
| Venus | Jupiter | Baths | Forum | Patricians |

Ancient Rome Bingo: Card No. 8

# Ancient Rome Bingo

| Greeks | Etruscans | Horace | Hadrian's Wall | Julius Caesar |
|--------|-----------|--------|----------------|---------------|
| Colosseum | Juno | Plebians | Forum | Neptune |
| Legion | Roman Empire | | Assemblies | Fauns |
| Epithets | Circus Maximus | Pluto | Pantheon | Insulae |
| Pompeii | Republic | Constantine I | Wardrobe | Mercury |

# Ancient Rome Bingo

| | | | | |
|---|---|---|---|---|
| Wardrobe | Mosaics | Ceres | Romulus | Hadrian's Wall |
| Vulcan | Cicero | Aqueducts | Assemblies | Juno |
| Punic Wars | Neptune | | Justinian | Diana |
| Pluto | Mercury | Epithets | Republic | Legion |
| Constantine I | Patricians | Minerva | Pax Romana | Plebians |

Ancient Rome Bingo: Card No. 10

# Ancient Rome Bingo

| Augustus | Neptune | Forum | Epithets | Patricians |
|---|---|---|---|---|
| Fauns | Legion | Pantheon | Greeks | Aqueducts |
| Mars | Juno | | Minerva | Horace |
| Constantine I | Aurora | Republic | Julius Caesar | Wardrobe |
| Colosseum | Jupiter | Roman Empire | Baths | Etruscans |

Ancient Rome Bingo: Card No. 11

# Ancient Rome Bingo

| Etruscans | Circus Maximus | Legion | Mosaics | Greeks |
|---|---|---|---|---|
| Horace | Patricians | Bacchus | Baths | Assemblies |
| Roman Empire | Insulae |  | Vulcan | Romulus |
| Jupiter | Pompeii | Juno | Wardrobe | Mars |
| Neptune | Fauns | Punic Wars | Colosseum | Cicero |

# Ancient Rome Bingo

| Epithets | Circus Maximus | Augustus | Legion | Vulcan |
|---|---|---|---|---|
| Bacchus | Fauns | Juno | Greeks | Diana |
| Mosaics | Cicero | | Horace | Insulae |
| Plebians | Republic | Ceres | Punic Wars | Wardrobe |
| Jupiter | Mercury | Baths | Roman Empire | Pantheon |

Ancient Rome Bingo: Card No. 13

# Ancient Rome Bingo

| | | | | |
|---|---|---|---|---|
| Julius Caesar | Juno | Forum | Greeks | Colosseum |
| Cicero | Roman Empire | Legion | Assemblies | Neptune |
| Epithets | Justinian | | Minerva | Constantine I |
| Mercury | Republic | Punic Wars | Ceres | Augustus |
| Jupiter | Romulus | Diana | Patricians | Plebians |

© Barbara M. Peller

# Ancient Rome Bingo

| Pantheon | Greeks | Forum | Etruscans | Mosaics |
|---|---|---|---|---|
| Augustus | Minerva | Aqueducts | Bacchus | Colosseum |
| Vulcan | Roman Empire |  | Aurora | Neptune |
| Jupiter | Legion | Fauns | Republic | Epithets |
| Patricians | Pompeii | Baths | Hadrian's Wall | Horace |

Ancient Rome Bingo: Card No. 15

# Ancient Rome Bingo

| | | | | |
|---|---|---|---|---|
| Ceres | Legion | Fauns | Hadrian's Wall | Roads |
| Romulus | Diana | Insulae | Mars | Justinian |
| Epithets | Circus Maximus | | Vulcan | Horace |
| Virgil | Cicero | Jupiter | Pantheon | Wardrobe |
| Colosseum | Senators | Baths | Pompeii | Neptune |

# Ancient Rome Bingo

| Constantine I | Ovid | Janus | Legion | Julius Caesar |
|---|---|---|---|---|
| Pantheon | Colosseum | Republic | Justinian | Insulae |
| Greeks | Plebians | | Senators | Fauns |
| Mercury | Patricians | Wardrobe | Forum | Diana |
| Pluto | Epithets | Etruscans | Mosaics | Circus Maximus |

Ancient Rome Bingo: Card No. 17

© Barbara M. Peller

# Ancient Rome Bingo

| | | | | |
|---|---|---|---|---|
| Hadrian's Wall | Punic Wars | Cicero | Epithets | Romulus |
| Neptune | Constantine I | Pluto | Vulcan | Colosseum |
| Greeks | Diana | | Janus | Bacchus |
| Circus Maximus | Aqueducts | Republic | Wardrobe | Minerva |
| Senators | Legion | Forum | Ovid | Augustus |

# Ancient Rome Bingo

| | | | | |
|---|---|---|---|---|
| Vulcan | Augustus | Legion | Fauns | Wardrobe |
| Pantheon | Mosaics | Neptune | Etruscans | Justinian |
| Ovid | Julius Caesar | | Assemblies | Aurora |
| Minerva | Senators | Pluto | Pompeii | Janus |
| Bacchus | Roads | Patricians | Plebians | Baths |

Ancient Rome Bingo: Card No. 19

© Barbara M. Peller

# Ancient Rome Bingo

| | | | | |
|---|---|---|---|---|
| Punic Wars | Ovid | Mosaics | Legion | Baths |
| Cicero | Horace | Mars | Pluto | Romulus |
| Circus Maximus | Insulae | | Virgil | Aqueducts |
| Pax Romana | Venus | Vesta | Pompeii | Senators |
| Sulla | Plebians | Roads | Wardrobe | Janus |

Ancient Rome Bingo: Card No. 20

# Ancient Rome Bingo

| Pantheon | Augustus | Mars | Legion | Pax Romana |
|---|---|---|---|---|
| Circus Maximus | Janus | Ceres | Fauns | Roman Empire |
| Diana | Patricians |  | Ovid | Forum |
| Pluto | Etruscans | Senators | Mercury | Plebians |
| Virgil | Roads | Baths | Constantine I | Pompeii |

Ancient Rome Bingo: Card No. 21

# Ancient Rome Bingo

| | | | | |
|---|---|---|---|---|
| Hadrian's Wall | Minerva | Janus | Bacchus | Epithets |
| Romulus | Mosaics | Aurora | Fauns | Assemblies |
| Cicero | Justinian | | Roman Empire | Insulae |
| Senators | Mercury | Pompeii | Aqueducts | Julius Caesar |
| Roads | Constantine I | Ovid | Diana | Mars |

# Ancient Rome Bingo

| Ceres | Ovid | Etruscans | Bacchus | Baths |
|---|---|---|---|---|
| Augustus | Punic Wars | Patricians | Pantheon | Aqueducts |
| Minerva | Epithets | | Vesta | Roman Empire |
| Diana | Roads | Senators | Constantine I | Pompeii |
| Pax Romana | Venus | Plebians | Pluto | Janus |

# Ancient Rome Bingo

| Ceres | Punic Wars | Julius Caesar | Ovid | Fauns |
|---|---|---|---|---|
| Janus | Baths | Mars | Romulus | Roman Empire |
| Insulae | Hadrian's Wall | | Epithets | Diana |
| Pax Romana | Vesta | Senators | Constantine I | Circus Maximus |
| Sulla | Virgil | Roads | Mosaics | Venus |

Ancient Rome Bingo: Card No. 24

© Barbara M. Peller

# Ancient Rome Bingo

| | | | | |
|---|---|---|---|---|
| Virgil | Mars | Ovid | Forum | Janus |
| Aqueducts | Circus Maximus | Pantheon | Ceres | Assemblies |
| Mercury | Fauns | | Vesta | Senators |
| Aurora | Pax Romana | Venus | Roads | Justinian |
| Baths | Julius Caesar | Cicero | Colosseum | Sulla |

Ancient Rome Bingo: Card No. 25

# Ancient Rome Bingo

| Janus | Ovid | Minerva | Romulus | Hadrian's Wall |
|---|---|---|---|---|
| Pluto | Mosaics | Fauns | Punic Wars | Ceres |
| Mercury | Vesta |  | Justinian | Virgil |
| Constantine I | Bacchus | Pax Romana | Roads | Senators |
| Insulae | Colosseum | Forum | Venus | Sulla |

Ancient Rome Bingo: Card No. 26

# Ancient Rome Bingo

| | | | | |
|---|---|---|---|---|
| Minerva | Cicero | Ovid | Punic Wars | Horace |
| Pax Romana | Vesta | Pantheon | Senators | Assemblies |
| Republic | Venus | | Roads | Virgil |
| Hadrian's Wall | Augustus | Mars | Sulla | Aqueducts |
| Colosseum | Justinian | Janus | Aurora | Insulae |

Ancient Rome Bingo: Card No. 27

# Ancient Rome Bingo

| | | | | |
|---|---|---|---|---|
| Ancient Rome | Punic Wars | Aurora | Ovid | Ceres |
| Horace | Janus | Vesta | Romulus | Justinian |
| Venus | Diana | | Insulae | Pluto |
| Wardrobe | Hadrian's Wall | Patricians | Roads | Senators |
| Bacchus | Greeks | Colosseum | Sulla | Pax Romana |

Ancient Rome Bingo: Card No. 28

© Barbara M. Peller

# Ancient Rome Bingo

| | | | | |
|---|---|---|---|---|
| Janus | Punic Wars | Hadrian's Wall | Pantheon | Greeks |
| Energy | Pluto | Mars | Insulae | Aurora |
| Mercury | Vesta | | Assemblies | Ovid |
| Horace | Pax Romana | Juno | Roads | Senators |
| Ceres | Fauns | Sulla | Augustus | Venus |

Ancient Rome Bingo: Card No. 29

# Ancient Rome Bingo

| Julius Caesar | Ovid | Romulus | Greeks | Senators |
|---|---|---|---|---|
| Aqueducts | Punic Wars | Minerva | Justinian | Assemblies |
| Mercury | Epithets |  | Insulae | Mars |
| Sulla | Augustus | Bacchus | Roads | Vesta |
| Pax Romana | Etruscans | Venus | Janus | Aurora |

Ancient Rome Bingo: Card No. 30

www.ingramcontent.com/pod-product-compliance
Lightning Source LLC
LaVergne TN
LVHW061337060426

835511LV00014B/1961